THIS WALKER BOOK BELONGS TO:

_____

_____

_____

_____

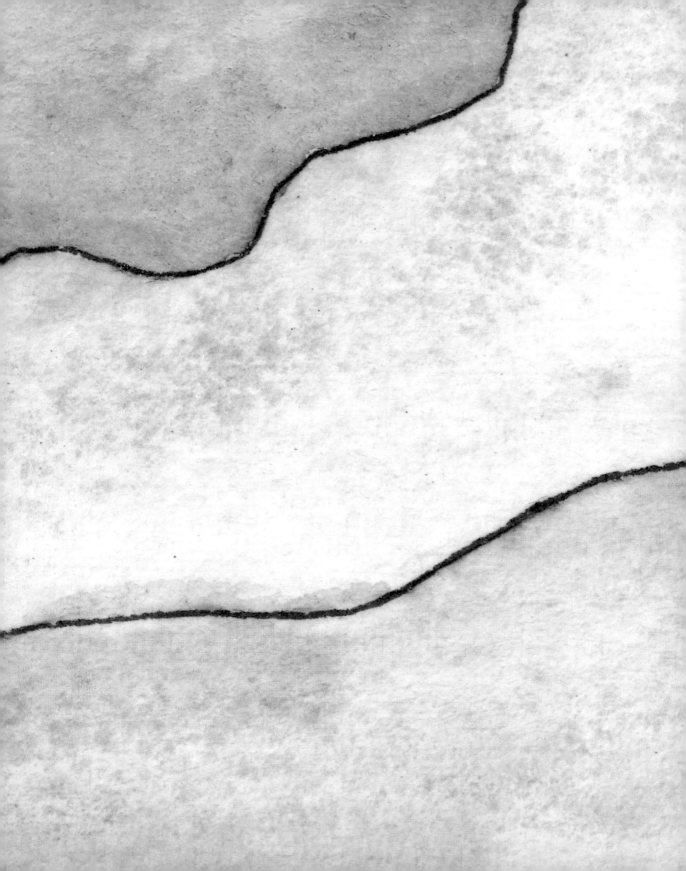

To Tudor, Araminta
and Rufus

First published 1987 by Walker Books Ltd
87 Vauxhall Walk, London SE11 5HJ

This edition published 1998

2 4 6 8 10 9 7 5 3 1

© 1987 Marcia Williams

Printed in Hong Kong/China

British Library Cataloguing in Publication Data
A catalogue record for this book is
available from the British Library.

ISBN 0-7445-6317-8

THE FIRST CHRISTMAS

Written and illustrated by
Marcia Williams

WALKER BOOKS
AND SUBSIDIARIES
LONDON · BOSTON · SYDNEY

Many, many days

and nights ago

in the far-off town of Nazareth,

a woman named Mary knelt in prayer.

An angel called Gabriel

came down in a cloud of golden light.

"Fear not, Mary, for God has favoured you.

You will bear a son and call him Jesus.

He will be great. His Kingdom will never end."

An angel also visited Joseph, Mary's betrothed,

to bring him the good news

and ask him to care for Mary and the baby.

Soon Mary and Joseph were married

and shared a great feast with their friends.

Then Joseph, who was a carpenter,

made a crib and wooden toys for Jesus.

Mary sewed swaddling clothes and blankets.

Soon all was ready for the birth.

But Jesus was not to be born at home.

The mighty Roman emperor ordered that

everyone should return to their home town

in order to pay their taxes.

Joseph's family came from Bethlehem,

seventy miles from Nazareth.

Although it was winter

and the baby was nearly due,

Joseph and Mary had to go to Bethlehem.

Sadly Mary packed the food

and mounted their donkey.

The journey to Bethlehem was long and tiring.

Some days were rainy and some were windy.

At night the air was bitterly cold.

It took Mary and Joseph several days ...

to reach the lights of Bethlehem.

In Bethlehem the streets were crowded.

There were many travellers

and all the inns were full.

Joseph knocked on one door,

then another, and another, and another.

But the answer was always the same –

"No room!" "No room!" "No room at the inn!"

Tears came to Mary's eyes.

Their donkey was very tired.

At last a kind innkeeper took pity on them.

He showed them to his stable.

"You can sleep here," he said.

"My ox and ass will keep you warm."

Mary and Joseph were very grateful.

They filled the manger with straw

to make a crib for Jesus.

Then they lay down to rest.

During the night the baby was born.

Meanwhile, in a field close by,

shepherds sat guarding their sheep.

All at once they heard singing.

The angel Gabriel descended into their midst.

The shepherds were terrified.

"Fear not," said Gabriel,

"for I bring you tidings of great joy.

Jesus our Saviour is born

this very night in Bethlehem."

The shepherds were very excited.

They left their sheep

and went into Bethlehem,

guided by a bright light.

There they found the baby Jesus

and knelt before him in wonder.

Three wise men from the East

saw a shining star.

They knew its meaning

and prepared to follow it

in search of the Son of God.

Caspar, Melchior and Balthazar

followed the star

for miles and miles

until at last ...

it led them to Bethlehem.

There they found Mary and Joseph

and the baby Jesus.

They knelt in worship, offering gifts

of gold, frankincense and myrrh.

The people of Bethlehem saw this

and also knelt in worship.

Young and old alike were filled with joy

now that Jesus their Saviour was born.

Since that day Christians all over the world

remember the birthday of Jesus.

We call this special day Christmas.

All over the world bells ring out.

People go to church to give thanks to God

for the birth of Jesus Christ.

At this happy time of year we sing carols

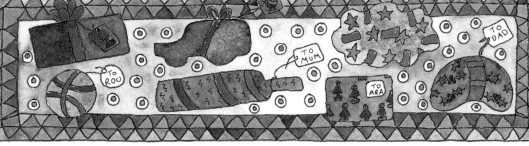

and give presents.

We invite our friends and family

to help us celebrate.

They join us for Christmas dinner

and we wish everyone

A

VERY

MERRY

CHRISTMAS

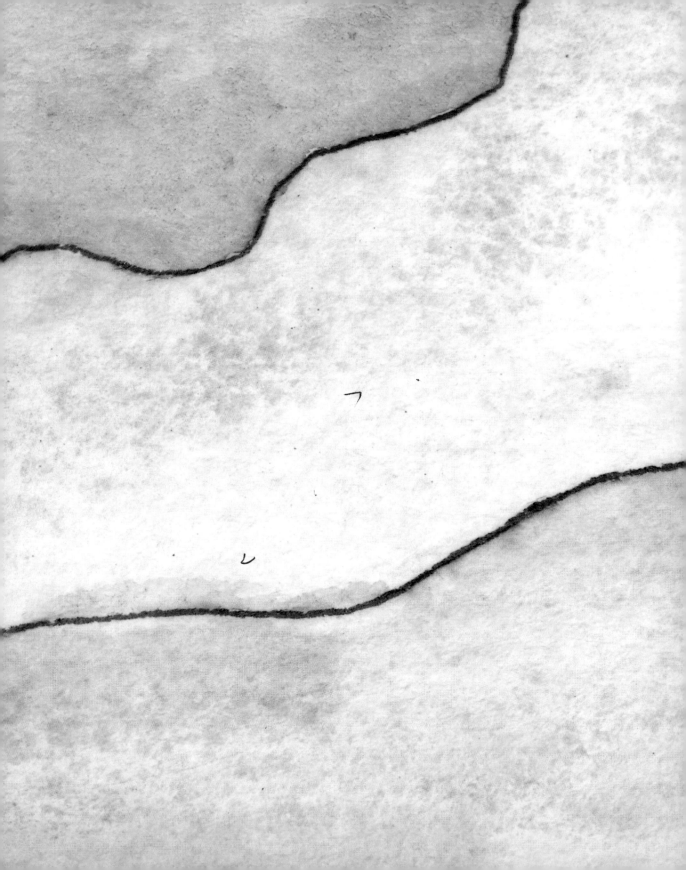

MORE WALKER PAPERBACKS
For You to Enjoy

Other Bible story retellings by Marcia Williams

THE AMAZING STORY OF NOAH'S ARK

The amazing story of Noah and his ark is one of the
world's greatest and best-loved tales.
Bright comic-strip illustrations and a simple text bring this
favourite Old Testament story to life for young children.

"Friendly, lively and intricate… Beautifully coloured borders."
The Observer

0-7445-6058-6   £4.99

JONAH AND THE WHALE

When Jonah disobeys God, he finds himself in the belly of an enormous whale!
More comic-strip Bible story fun.

"What makes Marcia Williams' version of the story so absorbing
are the wonderfully detailed and beautiful illustrations…
A picture book full of life and colour." *Child Education*

0-7445-6059-4   £4.99

JOSEPH AND HIS MAGNIFICENT COAT OF MANY COLOURS

Full of drama, incident and emotion, the adventures of Joseph
are as colourful as his glorious coat itself.

"Every page is awash with colour and detail…
Children will find much to enjoy here." *Child Education*

0-7445-6060-8   £4.99